House in Love Country

poems by

Patricia Bassel

Finishing Line Press
Georgetown, Kentucky

House in Love Country

Copyright © 2023 by Patricia Bassel
ISBN 979-8-88838-086-4 First Edition
All rights reserved under International and Pan-American Copyright Conventions. No part of this book may be reproduced in any manner whatsoever without written permission from the publisher, except in the case of brief quotations embodied in critical articles and reviews.

ACKNOWLEDGMENTS

I treasure the many summers I spent at the Taos and Sante Fe Summer Writers' Conferences immersing myself in the poetry world. Inspiration still comes from my mentors there—Luci Tapahonso, Joy Harjo, Valerie Martinez, Stephen Benz, Richard Vargas and Greg Glazner. A special thanks to Sawnie Morris for her interest and encouragement in the creative writing process and for finding a story in my poems. Grateful for these publications: *Third Street Writers* for including "We Were Three Women in a City of Water," *Hey I'm Alive* for "dear friend," *Unstamatic* for "Dusk," *Oklahoma Today Magazine* for "Am I Blue?" A heartfelt thanks to family and friends who inspire me with their ideas, their conversations, their stories and their warm spirit.

Publisher: Leah Huete de Maines
Editor: Christen Kincaid
Cover Art: Russell Bassel
Author Photo: Brian Birdwell
Cover Design: Elizabeth Maines McCleavy

Order online: www.finishinglinepress.com
 also available on amazon.com

Author inquiries and mail orders:
Finishing Line Press
P. O. Box 1626
Georgetown, Kentucky 40324
U. S. A.

Table of Contents

Love County

House in Love County 1
In the Evening He Reads His Way into the Next Dream 3
Under a January Moon 4
On Children Playing Outside 5
Day at the Park 6
Letters from Dad 7
Corner Booth 8
Awakening 9
Leaving for Korea 10

Across Borders

Motorcycle Ride 13
I Remember What Came Next Completely 14
Nietzsche's Path 16
Why Have a Dog? 17
How Was Paris 18
In Oklahoma 20
Some Kind of Permanence 21
Offering 23
Sometimes the Darkness Would Tie Me Down 24
Drums of Duende 25

Love's Return

Dwell in Beauty 29
I Was Reading 30
A Story of Afghans 31
Psalm to the Crescent Moon 32

Dusk 33
Love Letter 34
May Third, Corn Dance 35
Brave Ones 36
Pecking at the Winter Grass 37
Dear Picture Postcard 39
Rock of Ages 40
Daybreak on Mount Scott 42
In This House 43
Bouquet of Basil 44

Postscript: **Dear Friends**
Three Women in a City of Water 47
Whispers of Old Kyoto 48
Tears for Betty Friedan 49
dear friend 50
Desert Nocturne 51
Long Live Liberace 52
Herb Garden 53
Reunión 54
Am I Blue? 55
In a Chagall Painting 56

*For the memory of my parents
who connected me to books*

*For the memory of my grandparents
who connected me to the earth*

To Brian for letting in the sun

"It's raining women's voices as if they had died even in memory
And it's raining you as well marvellous encounters of my life
O little
drops"
—Apollinaire, *Calligrammes Poèmes de la Paix et de la Gùerre 1918*
Translated by Roger Shattuck

Love County

"How many more times will you remember a certain afternoon of your childhood, some afternoon that's so deeply a part of your being that you can't even conceive of your life without it?"
—Paul Bowles, *The Sheltering Sky*

House in Love County

In a box is a photograph. I notice the curve
of Papa's smile. He sits on the porch paying little attention to tangled
honeysuckle bushes and the scurry of grasshoppers. The top of his head is lost
under a broad-brimmed straw hat. I live for a moment in his shadow
wanting to sit on his lap where life is simple, and the bitter
taste of a cucumber, green and tender, is not a distant

memory. The paint on his rocking chair is weathered. Other towns are distant,
faraway places. This is Love County, Oklahoma, a curve
in the road that leads to open spaces. Only a few trucks drive by with their bitter
exhaust, and the grandchildren with their tangled
hair and soft giggles wave to say hello. They laugh at their own shadows
in the afternoon sun. Is this tender thread of childhood lost

when grandfathers have left their front porches? Children get lost
in their desire to break free and run to the distant
pasture. The grass is taller than they are. An oak tree casts its shadow.
Grandmother is calling. The children run down the curved,
grassy path to the house with no plumbing. The excitement of their words gets tangled in a
story about the thrill of the outside—a blue, gold, bitter-

sweet day, that can't last forever. The orange peel is bitter
against the tongue that catches playful language soon to be lost
in cities and heavy traffic, crowded places tangled
in high-pitched noises and shouting voices where a distant
cry from the country longs to be heard again. A curve
to the left and then to the right leads to a familiar shadow

captured in the sunlight. What is different now is the shadow
goes unnoticed. I am too busy on this bitter
cold day in January. It takes warmth on a summer day in the country where the curve in the
road leads to truth again. Nothing has been lost.
The urge is still there to take off my shoes and run to a distant
field. I leave behind the day's quickened pace. My mind becomes untangled,

unfettered. I am no longer backed in the corner. I am like an insect tangled
in a web that suddenly breaks free. We weave a pattern of mystical shadows.
The light is on Papa's face. His smile is distant,
but radiant. The light fades in and out. A bitter
storm gives way to soft breezes. I have not lost
my sense of direction. I slow down. I linger and I wonder if around the curve

are the tangled vines of the honeysuckle. I wish the chill from the bitter wind and the dark shadows would go away. The days on the front porch are not lost. Lights cast a beam on the curve in the road. The house on the hill is in the distance.

In the Evening He Reads His Way into the Next Dream
(father at 75)

where I whisper a fairy tale that will be lost in memory.
He is not too old to see the beauty of moving fish under murky water,
the overgrown garden bathed in midsummer sunshine,
or the children's stories in which he recognizes his own.
When the music of Borodin's *Prince Igor* swells on the radio,
he breathes in every intricate, hard-earned musical note.
But the arms that once lifted me in the air are paler.
They lack the color of summer on the combine,
the energy that reached for paint on his palette in winter,
the strength that carried the heavy load of detailed planning
for camping trips in summer. Autumn pulls him from the world around me
like a leaf that dangles from the tree. It doesn't hold on to the branch forever.

Under a January Moon

my mother slipped away from winter's
slumber to take the stage of summer.
Dipper lights dimmed
as the curtain of early morning opened
on my mother sipping coffee
and resting on the back patio.

If that mockingbird don't sing,
Momma's gonna buy you a diamond ring.

I heard
the sound of the screen door,
the sprinkler on the herb garden,
(where the garlic still grows)
the rustle of the newspaper being read
with all those words (not needed now)
only the simple "I love you."
On summer mornings she sang to me

If that mockingbird don't sing,
Momma's gonna buy you a diamond ring.

The morning after a thunderstorm
she plucked the petals of a marguerite,
"he loves me, he loves me not,
he loves me passionately."
A bouquet of wildest dreams she offered me
in a backyard of rose of Sharon, pampas grass, and marigolds.

"If that mockingbird don't sing,
Momma's gonna buy you a diamond ring."

in memory of marguerite spencer bassel
august 3, 1914—january 24, 2008

On Children Playing *Outside*

Outside the air smells of damp earth and dirt.
Honeybees gather on clover. There's the chance of getting stung.
Outside I see the driveway with a rainbow designed in chalk.
And a big round yellow sun, rays shooting out.
She even signs her name in blue *outside*. It will fade and disappear
like the early morning dewdrops in June, while the sprinkler sings *outside*.
There is a sudden afternoon thunderstorm, the thrill of lightning bolts—
I dash to check the mailbox, then find shelter on the porch,
my hair wet with rain. There's a tornado siren.
Dark clouds. Then the storm subsides. Next door
two sisters turn their imperfected cartwheels, ragdoll hair and feet.
A recess break from homeschool in their fenced front yard, protected.
Their mother listens to police reports and weather alerts *outside*.
A robin gathers winter's dead grass, flies off with the bounty.
There's a basketball hoop, a kid's wading pool, a soccer ball.
There are bicycles to take off for Numu Creek, a place for picnics.
There is a sound, *a tempo* of feet hitting the backyard trampoline.
There is a Billie Holiday song in the low-pitched hum of children's chatter.
Night falls with goodbyes and out-of-breath sighs *outside*, "God Bless the Child."

A Day at the Park

A mother sits on the grass with a child in her arms.
Picnic tables sprawl under trees.
She has found refuge in the park away from dirty dishes, unmade beds.
She likes the way sun-rays come sliding in over tree tops.
Day comes to life around her,
rich with crepitating noises and a strong, sweet, wafting scent of jasmine.
She remembers a hurried breakfast, a curt conversation between two people
separated by a Formica tabletop and recirculating air.
In her thoughts she will leave him.
She will make a new home— visit her mother in August,
get a rescue dog, get rid of the Sango china. But where will she live?
How will she get a job? Would going back to school satisfy her hunger?
A multitude of questions rush through her in a pounding discord,
leaving her anxious as she reaches in her purse for a notepad and pen.
She lets her child play with a rabbit's foot while she makes a list.
She will write it down and keep it for herself as she would a treasured letter.
Then something happens, something magical,
and the tension goes out of her.
It has to do with the wish list and the grass, its dampness, its coolness,
the way it conforms to her toes, her arches, her heels.
The wind massages her. She has it on paper now.
She puts the list and amulet back in her purse.
Hand in hand she and her child walk back home.

Letters from Dad

Were all your letters suns, I could not see one.
The artistry of ink to paper escaped me.
I ignored the slow, deliberate pause of your punctuation,
the subtlety of your stories on ivory leaves.
Could I follow your lead and sit at the desk by the window and capture the sun?

I lived in a cloud of darkness not noticing while you brushed
your feather-plume-quill into a detailed portrait of love.
Rivers gather stones, bit by bit. Like that,
I slowly came to discover your words.

Corner Booth

as i ate honey on my sopapilla

   it dripped down my chin
   it stuck to my fingers
   it felt like glue
   (actually more like the fun of bubble gum, of mud in my shoes)
   it tasted sweet and naughty
   it gave me a thrill
   it melted in my mouth

I forgot about it being late and how tired I was from the long drive through barren country
hollis, oklahoma
& on to texas towns
memphis
amarillo
dumas
delhart
springer
& deserted roads
new mexico's
cimarron

I sit in the corner booth and watch families
   eat tortillas, chalupas, enchiladas, frijoles, tacos
   talk about the powwow
   sip summer ice tea

as I eat honey on my sopapilla

july 13, 2007
michael's kitchen
taos, new mexico

Awakening

It started out as a time-consuming process, the creation of a derivative notebook in Latin class. A notebook to feature the vocabulary of base words that expand on the horizon with prefixes and suffixes adding sunrises and sunsets to the long days and nights. Pages and pages of black ink poured out words like pugnacious, amorous, amorist, vortex, quintessential—revealing their core, their true nature while I was still searching for mine as I looked at the world through a dictionary.

But the words blossomed into stories of Vercingetorix putting up a good fight before Julius Caesar conquered Gaul. I met a resistance fighter. *Pugnare.*

History came alive and the world revealed its quintessential essence through the four elements of earth, air, fire, water. After conjugating verbs we took field trips to Paris and the provinces. I stood awestruck as I gazed upon the statue of Vercingetorix on a sunny afternoon in the vortex of Alesia.

june 24, 2015

Leaving for Korea

My cat Gypsy was in good hands.
My friend Hillary would take her in.
My sister with the green thumb
would love my plants.
I was clearing the rented duplex on Columbia Street—
one bedroom, one bath,
detached garage.

Lots of quiet conversation
had taken place
on the big front porch
in Old Town North.
Gypsy had birthed four kittens
in the back of the closet.
I knew the park down the street
with monkey bars and a merry-go-round
and the young couple next door.
I taught French at a high school
only four blocks away.

I check the atlas.
Pusan, South Korea is 6671 miles,
from the Wichitas and prairie grass
from Medicine Bluff (Puha Tupana) and Medicine Creek
where Comanches once hunted.
Will I ever feel this close to the spirit of a place?

Across Borders

"What is that feeling when you're driving away from people and they recede on the plain till you see their specks dispersing? It's the too huge world vaulting us and it's goodbye. But we lean forward to the next crazy venture beneath the skies."
—Jack Kerouac, *On the Road*

Motorcycle Ride

I take a motorcycle ride through Old San Juan.
A glossy white helmet engulfs my head
not heavy like my boots. Leather gloves
envelop my sweaty hands holding on to his waist
the way a child hugs a tree branch when happy—
with an edge—far from the ground.
My heart is racing with the thrill of laughter,
the revving up of playful conversation
against the rage of the motorcycle roar on hot pavement.

I leave you—
slow crawl of Sunday in the country,
lazy morning on the porch,
drawn out note held in the moonlight of Thelonius Monk.

I abandon you—
silky white lace dresses in pristine places
where I never wanted to live,
where conversation droned on as I closed my eyes in a slumber
dreaming of rough terrain, slippery rocks and long ladders
leading to caves that cling to the ocean's margin.

I live here now—
where the wind hits my face
unsure of the next cobbled-stone
swerve, leaning in left, side by side with sun-drenched *apartamentos*
where music pours out on the crowded street
on to the *Plaza San Cristóbal*, where two old men smoke
in the afternoon heat. A warm breeze rustles
the mango leaves. Water spews from the fountain
as children gather and kick a soccer ball down the narrow
streets of Old San Juan, where—

I ride.

I Remember What Came Next Completely

Sitting at the *Charles de Gaulle airport*
south of the city of light, early morning,
I think about the city I am leaving,
artists waking up to gargoyles glistening in the sun,
city sweepers at work, waiters unstacking wicker bistro tables
and chairs so close shoulders will touch,
the noise of a delivery truck drowning out quiet conversations
between sips of espresso. *A brief pause in the story.*

I wake from my reverie to the sound of
passengers, dazed as they walk
down the long corridor of Terminal 2.
They comb their hair, read the newspaper,
a woman fumbles through her purse for lipstick.
Flights arrive from LAX, JFK, Atlanta.
The airport explodes into a city of strangers
like the corner bar where the lonely mingle,
but on a much larger scale. A glance may bring a smile.
Two people face to face nod and say hello.
I wonder what their story is.

I remember what came next completely. I recognized
TV journalist Andy Rooney and his wife
grabbing a suitcase from the luggage carousel.
They looked in their sixties, packs on their backs.
They had the casual look of seasoned travelers
in comfortable shoes to walk along the Seine,
stop at *Shakespeare and Company* for books,
load up the backpacks, include some cheese
and olives from the *Marché Rue de Buci*,
read a few pages of the *International Herald Tribune*,
gaze into each other's eyes at the *Café Contrescarpe*.
He laces his fingers through her thick gray hair.
(This is my version of their story).

Turns out
His wife's name was Marguerite.
He lived to be 92. She 84.

They were married 62 years.
He reported his 60 Minutes commentary at a walnut desk
which he had made himself
where he talked of trivia, the details of daily life—
the price of eggs, Christmas ties, the overflowing junk drawer, pets that wear clothes, annoying relatives, bottled water brands—

And they came to Paris once
traveling like me.

february 19, 2016

Nietzsche's Path

Sometimes I think about Nietzsche's path on the outskirts of Nice
winding its way up to Eze on the Grande Corniche
where I picked wild rosemary.
Did Nietzsche wander down the same narrow streets of the *vieille ville*
and taste *socca* sprinkled with black pepper
wrapped in cone-shaped paper
made fresh to order straight out of the wood-burning oven?
I was teaching English at the *Lycée du Parc Impérial,*
a school that was up the hill from the Mediterranean Sea.
I found poetry that year.
Apollinaire, Jacques Prévert, Paul Éluard filled my head
five years after my divorce.

When I unpacked my two suitcases after the night train from Paris to Nice
(too excited to get much sleep in my *couchette*),
I thought of Stein, Colette, Simone de Beauvoir.
(Would they come later in my life)?
"I am giddy, expectation whirls me 'round,"
Shakespeare said.

What matters is I came to Nice in my thirties,
left a secure job and Columbia Street
for ten months abroad
where poetry prevailed.
I wanted to feel alive!
Liberté
J'écris ton nom.

Where shall I walk on a sunny afternoon now?
Pick a tree-lined street.
Think back to the first dance,

the fast ride on the playground's merry-go-round,
head thrown back,
gravel making a mosaic on the ground like
sprigs of wild rosemary along Nietzsche's path.

Why have a Dog?

Why have a dog on a day like this
when a truck runs people down on the streets of Nice
and the destruction amid a Bastille crowd
takes the forefront to the backdrop
beauty of the sea.

Why have a dog on a day like this?

Willie, a seven-pound poodle, runs into the dog park
like a third grader, hits the playground at
10:30 a.m. (freedom after spelling)
reminding me *here* is where democracy exists.
The smallest dog is on equal ground
with German shepherds, a golden lab, a Great Pyrenees,
The pack huddles together on the big expanse of land.
If it were hot august summer, Willie would be
the sunburned boy revving up at the edge
jumping cannonball into the pool
hungry for the sting, the spray, the smell of water.
Instead he's stirring up the settled dust
rolling over and over,
his curly coat covered in dirt.
I watch his joy from leafy shadows.
Willie, reverting back to wolf,
walks and wanders without a leash.
Released from his work day, solitude and long daily naps,
Willie lives his dream of going to Pamplona
and running with the bulls.

How Was Paris

it's 4 o'clock in the morning
and a 4-hour train ride from paris
where the 2 of us walked along the *rue mouffetard*

i remember
    a saxophone player
    bringing blues to the *île saint-louis*
    a woman leaning on the trunk of the cedar of lebanon
    the beauty of age   a black scarf
    hiding her hair
    but not her dreamy gaze
    by the labyrinth
    of the *jardin des plantes*

we there
    lingering
    in bookshops and music stores

we discover
    rue du trésor
    macarons fresh, warm to our touch

i awaken to
    heartbeat noises of the 5th arrondissement
    church bells of *saint-étienne-du-mont*
    footsteps along the *rue Descartes*

Our day is full of varied rhythms,
    the high and low of voices along the *rue clovis*
    the squeal of mopeds
    the rapid loud rush of students who take to the streets
    boul' mich alive with protests
    is love worth fighting for is love worth dying for is freedom worth war

you say
    impeach bush
i say
    free tibet

    breathing in the past and the present

you picked
> the arena of lutetia for our picnic
> (what more could i ask for)
> paris was this is this and more *mon amour*

> in paris

we are
> lovers holding hands along the seine
> moving on and on like the river

notre dame
> is a beautiful woman
> her bellringer is a rebel

2008

In Oklahoma

where there's peace
in holding on and letting go
my mother died in a nursing home
4 months before you took me to paris in april
with pink blossom promises and a light snow

it's only now 2 years later when people ask me
   how was paris

i can say
   beautiful

2010

Some Kind of Permanence

Day 1
You took me out of the confines of my routine out of the rolling hills of Germany
to the flatlands of Familie den Braven Buitenhaven 10 2965 Ae Nieuwpoort

the Netherlands brave.heart@wxs. nl. bed and breakfast "de Uitspanning"
…which in my American way means reaching out— out

where the Lek River passes through fields of windmills
where a shepherd herds his goats to graze on the grass of the dykes

I remember the footpath at dusk at Kinderdijk,
the backdrop of windmills and thatched roofs

We followed the trail with cameras and curiosity
for a closer view of people who live in windmills

and work their gardens in wooden shoes
They waved at us…their gate opened

curious about the other side we took the ferry across the River Lek
to Schoonhoven where we found silver and gold

and curious heart-shaped shrubs in a front yard
only 1 euro for 2 on a ferry

Day 2
We spent an afternoon in Amsterdam where we breathed in the sweet smell
behind the Doors Coffee Shop Spuistraat 46 on the Singel

We inhaled the garden of sculptured iguanas, komodo dragons, and tattered tulips
and exhaled the pissoirs, the trams, Rembrandt, Amsterdam

Night 2
Out of the sexy, noisy neon city
we walked the dark, cobblestoned streets of Nieuwpoort
past what I call a cottage with a *Te Koop* (for sale) sign
enough light and laughter inside

to lure us for a moment
like typical American shoppers at a window who want to possess

we continued (late night walks are our anodyne)
and finally sat on a dyke and watched boats along the River Lek

we're comfortable with movement—
windmills, our steps, ripples in water

Day 3
I remember our laughter at breakfast.
Before we left

I signed the guest book
marked with a flower

to ink in some kind of permanence
below sea level on top of the world.

april 2007

Offering

I like how the farmer slices apples for tasting
at the market early Saturday
morning, placing them on a dark wooden cutting
board with toothpicks. He knows their crispness, their burst
of juice, like honey on the tongue. I'm paused—
on my way to meet the excavation technician
and musician whom I need to forget.
He no longer meets me to walk me home
after movies (which he didn't attend).
I love that old cinema art house in the
heart of the Altstadt, its red velvet curtains,
its lush chairs, the winding staircase, art nouveau.
I am caught amid October's harvest,
scent of fresh bread and coffee perfumes the air.
Maybe I know—in this moment of
staying for the offering of apples—what is about to come. No
more nights spent attending his concerts. No
more moonlight walks with a stop at the corner
café, his dog Jalkie lying at our feet.
I choose the Jonathan Gold. Gold of autumn
sunlight. Like the apple trees that dazzle in
the daylight along the highway winding its way
through the Taunus Mountains. I think of that June
when my sister and I drove south across the
Red River into Texas to buy Charlie
peaches. We stopped at a stand beside an orchard
on the edge of town with no one around.
I remember baskets brimming with peaches,
and the sign that stated, *Take a few. One dollar, please.*
(A small price to pay for one of summer's pleasures.)

Sometimes the Darkness Would Tie Me Down

I would have to turn a corner
from this place, my flat, my home on Arndt Strasse. A milestone—
like the pilgrim reaching *Santiago de Compostela*.
I couldn't stay
in the same place. Sometimes the darkness
would tie me down. Blindfold me.
I couldn't see the stars,
prairie blazing star wildflowers,
Chagall's brushstrokes of the redheaded mermaid midair,
the tallest book in a crammed bookcase   *Heart of Darkness*.
I lost sight of the blonde   upright piano,
birds in formation,
the spider plant spilling over with new life.

Now I lay me down to sleep in a hospital bed
counting falling stars
without looking back at the sett stone street
where trees sprinkled pink blossoms in spring,
on the corner   a pub   tables outside   two glasses of wine,
a short walk away, the park, its benches.

Now I lay me down to sleep.
I am imagining Medicine Bluff,
that other place (Apaches call it holy ground)
light years from the stars,
scissortails on telephone wires,
to the east Sitting Bear Creek
where I pray the lord my soul to keep.

january 15, 2016

Drums of Duende

(*anglo* to *manito*)
how can I paint the landscape?
step among the sunflowers, feel the earth between your toes.

Will I remember the songs my mother gave me?
travel far and wide.
listen to children.
see the hawk in the afternoon sky.

Do I need music every day?
you told me your brother loves opera and spoke to you of the elixir of love
you love jazz, fado and Mexican boleros.
listen to the wind, patricia,
the ethnic wailing….

I laugh, weep, and sing when I read the letters he wrote me.
Will his words ever leave me?
hum, strum with the mariachi divas, patricia,
and keep their rhythm…

taos, new mexico 2010

Love's Return

"On the day when it will be possible for woman to love not in her weakness but in her strength, not to escape herself but to find herself, not to abuse herself but to assert herself—on that day love will become for her, as for man, a source of life..."
—Simone de Beauvoir, *The Second Sex*

Dwell in Beauty

She has lost sight of the damp green clover patch
and the tiny wildflowers that brightened her toes.
She does not want the bouquet of silk roses,
the sensible decorum inside expensive homes.

Instead her finger follows a smooth stem to her childhood
where the water quenches insatiable thirst
for cricket sounds, piñon smells, sagebrush.
Her story flows like the water
and seeps down the stones of limestone caves
where strong hands wrap around her.
She can live where ancient stories dwell in beauty
like blackbirds on sunflowers in summer.
She has the sweet taste of honeybee medicine on her tongue.

When she thinks it's too dark,
she will follow the path her father painted
on which the mother planted and received trees.
She'll find fragments of coral and turquoise
as small as mustard seeds.

When winter comes she will see blades of grass
in the snow. She will wander in the warmth of
his spirit wrapped in the quilt of bluestem dreams.

October 3, 2009

I Was Reading

an article about Friendship Benches in Zimbabwe
when my cat started making biscuits
on my chest. He wrinkled the pages with his paws.
I was already too intrigued in what was titled
"A Humble Solution to Global Depression,"
to set the article aside or leave it for the pile "maybe later."
Woodrow purred and burrowed down in human pillow.
We were comfortable on the couch in winter. I felt warm
from a cup of oolong tea, the fire, the furry cat. I learned that the term
for depression in Shona is *kufungisisa* which to natives means
"thinking too much."

I remembered a summer of ECT and thinking too much.

Van Gogh   Sylvia Plath   Edgar Allan Poe
come to mind as Woodrow's claws pinch through my jeans.
I have often seen him sharpen them on backyard tree trunks.
He needs them to hold his prey and climb. My hand
strokes the head of this once homeless creature.

I could see naked branches out my window and thought
about a wooden friendship bench under the shade of a tree—
where an elderly woman wearing a broad-brimmed hat sits under the African sun.
People call her *ambuya utano*, community grandmother. She talks
to a troubled girl   listening to the *cri de coeur*.
She is old but holds magic. She is there like a sunflower stalk, the sober,
hardworking trunk. The young woman seeking advice is her red-
flowered Moulin Rouge, smooth, delicate petals that need the sun.

I remembered one morning when I was reading on my back patio—
grape hyacinths made a carpet of misty blue—a gray tabby cat soon to have wood in his
name appeared. He was looking for a home.

A Story of Afghans

—for sally

1. She crocheted an afghan
for her granddaughter's wedding gift,
a family keepsake, handmade,
the year the U.S. and Cuba tied the knot,
the year Pope Francis visited America.
Angela Merkel smiled on a million Syrian refugees.
Terrorists attacked the Bataclan Concert Hall in Paris,
weeks later stormed an office party, San Bernadino.
She worked at home in her chair
untangling the yarn from the cat's clutches
or at sunlit cafes with other women.
She relished the everyday, consistently showing up
like a striker working the picket line.
Love's labor required her concentration,
a meditation on innocence
and young love blossoming.

2. In this house
I retrieve another afghan
from the top shelf of the closet,
black and white, cats on fences.
I touch, unfold and admire
this handmade gift from my mother.

She taught school, had a garden,
taught me how to swim, how to stay afloat.

I imagine a day in August—
her long wet hair, her suntanned skin,
a glass of cold lemonade.

She comes to me in bits and pieces
like a puzzle. A beach towel. An afghan.
My summer. My winter moon.

Psalm to the Crescent Moon

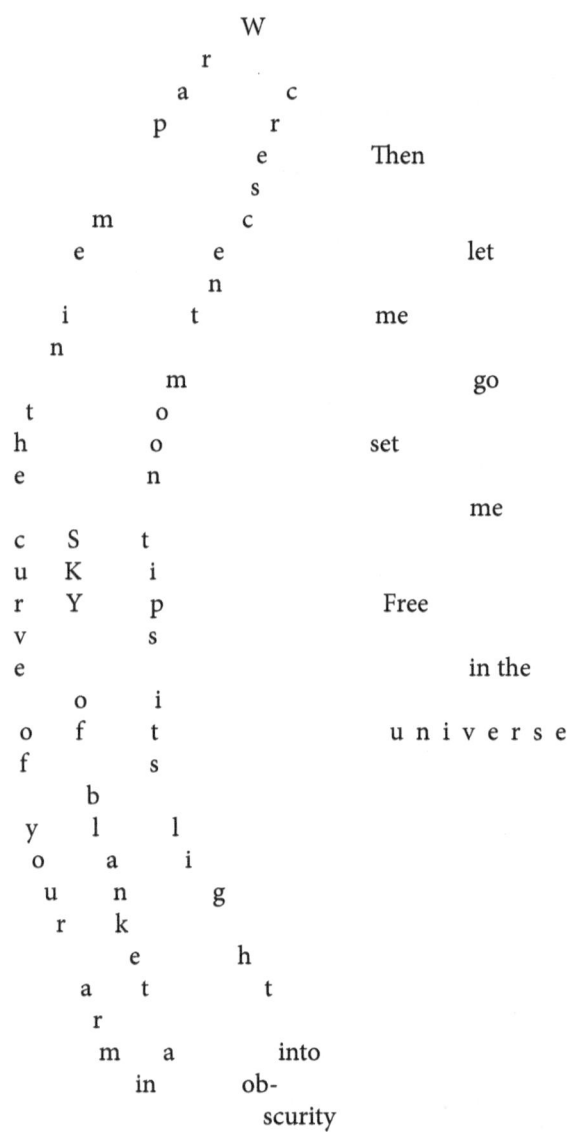

...my psalm abbreviated as I sip african coffee in the cat-clawed armchair. my father's "backyard in truchas" (1975) adorns the wall. /civil servant/technical writer/at a desk 9-5/ loved books/ art/growing grapes/purple martins/vacations. /"he restoreth my soul."

Dusk

Luc Bat poem for my sister Sarah

Pink-rimmed clouds in the sky,
Oklahoma dusk. Write a song,
a prayer, a page for Todd
who loved nature—rugged, free, strong—
lived in the country, longed
for scissortails, not wrong to die
on green grass where he lies—
long hair, tanned hands, closed eyes, alone
my sister's son who rode
the wave of prairie grass. Moon rise.

in memoriam
stephen todd wiseman
march 4, 1965-june 14, 2019

Love Letter

dear roxanne, maddy, lucy, aurie,
while you dance your way in and out of youth
learning hop scotch, ballet, ice hockey, karate,
cheerleading jumps, the moon gives off
just enough light to see the road before daybreak.
i walk the road up mt scott twice a week
to see the sunrise. i like
the 2.8-mile ascent, the view from the top,
the ancient boulders dotted with bright yellow lichen.
painted buntings leave mexico and central america to live in the wichitas
in may, june, july. i listen for their song.
they color the landscape like you design your tattoos—
  fire orange
    indigo
      sapphire
        lime
          yellow
you add a black & white joan miró that shouts—
We Belong in the World.
you live in wild honeysuckle— tangled, unruly.
you walk beside long-stemmed grasses with their brown
furry thick ends, cattails billowing, surviving in the wind.
you stir up dust like broncos of the rodeo
with your half-shaved head, meltdowns, rebellion.

i love you,
  roxanne
    maddy
      lucy
        aurie

like i do the bottlenose dolphin that every two hours sheds its skin.

May Third, Corn Dance

at the pueblo by red willow river
people gather for the corn dance.
i am not allowed to bring my camera or cell phone.
i purchase my ten-dollar ticket and honor the rules.
i walk the dirt path past the cemetery to the gathering.
blue corn tortillas, fry bread with honey are for sale, cold drinks and trinkets,
prayer sticks, a chakra chair carved out of cedar
where i can sit with my face toward the sun
and the bald eagle with the turquoise eye behind my back.
i rest for a while on the low walking bridge
that connects open space to adobe homes.
i dangle my feet and listen to the rush of stream water, the rio pueblo.
life is unhurried, time slithers away,
clouds move faster than people.
a girl with bare brown skin sits and reads along the water's edge.
a young man with a long black ponytail,
brushing the pocket of his jeans, waits.

the elders
    climb
        ladders.
strong profiles that were hidden behind dark adobe walls
    rise
        against sky
and soar with their eagle feathers.

they stand proud like Faunus over the forest,
one with the landscape,
protectors of dreams, visions in the wild
and celebrations for a bountiful harvest.

the time is after the birthing.
the sounds are distant drumbeats and heart whisperings.
the corn dancers begin to chant
and let loose their dancing feet.

Tahsua

Brave Ones

This is the place I want to be with
You
Rugged grassy path in the
Bosk
Our first time in the Osage
Hills
Trees offer shade but don't block
Sky
We are out of breath, taking
Steps
Over dead branches brittle
Brown
Like the earth, gold with autumn's
Leaves
Weightless, delicate, wet with
Dew
Morning tears that we carry with
Us
Sky & eyes cerulean
Two
Bodies in Picasso blue
Brave
We are to walk this aisle
Bare
Stripped down, nothing left but
Truth

Pecking at the Winter Grass

I like movies
on a Sunday
night when we scoot
our chairs together.
Share chocolate
chips. I love
your easy smile,
your tortoise-shell
glasses, curly hair.
We cry at movies.
The other night
you made me
laugh again
& again
so many
eye sparkles
I've lost count
because it's
not about
keeping score
or taking note
of grievances.
It's about
the napkin note
on the table.
the peck
on the cheek,
late night shrimp
on the grill.
how you create
our marinade.
We sit on your porch
We would like
a vegetable garden
so we build
our compost.

So many mornings
I've wanted to throw
on sweatpants,

a t-shirt and run
until my heart beats
fast and I sweat
fear out of
my pores. I reach
for coffee instead.
I see a blackbird
out my kitchen
window, yellow
beak pecking
at the winter
grass. I hold
out my arms
to your children.
Memento mori.
You jokingly speak
of my insouciance
when I get giddy
about traveling.
We giggle.
Let's rake our
Leaves. Add them
To the compost.
some days
I color us pensive
like a carambola
poppy salad.
Other days more daring
like a Ghanian
Kente cloth print.
We study
the pieces of us
like we would a Minoan mosaic
five thousand parts
to make a
whole.

Dear Picture Postcard,

            I remember the first time I saw you—
aged, with a coffee stain, but no creases around the edges.
Among the pile of torn and crumpled paper trash,
you stood out.
            It was in the heat of an Oklahoma summer
that I spotted you—a picture of soft-breeze dandelions
touched by unknown hands on one side. Nothing
written on the other side. I chose to keep you to write:
           I hear the pitter, patter of rain on the rooftop.
I smell the bouquet of crimson roses
that arrived unexpectedly after a hard knock
on the front door. Elvis Costello's Secret, Profane
and Sugarcane roars in the background like
loud thunder from the summer storm.

july 2011
taos

Rock of Ages

The *griot* smiles and tells his story of a polished tiger eye rock—
smooth, safe, all the rough edges washed away. "The tiger's eye
is a gift," he says, "created to ward off the evil eye."

I get the power of rocks.
They tell the story of the earth.
They rock my world.

I biked down Lincoln Street full speed ahead.
I played tether ball on the playground.
I read Khalil Gibran's *The Prophet*.
I took the bus from Alajuela to a country school for Spanish classes.
I biked down Biebrich Allee to the Rhine River.
I rode in a van on a rocky road in Ghana headed for Kpatave Middle School.

I was 6
  I was 12
    I was 30
      I was 42
        I was 56
          I was 68

We celebrate our newborns in the world.
We honor the sun, the flowing waters, the trees.
The Day of the Dead is our remembrance.

I understand why the song *My Favorite Things* makes me think of my brother's laughter.
I understand why home-grown tomatoes make me think of my mother's gazpacho.
I understand why a black ink pen makes me think of my father's letters.

I like to hike among the rocks.

People call it the "Wichita Uplift"
when mountains formed from rock
320 million years ago.
I am from the ancestral Rockies, the Wichitas.

I am at home in the world of
scissortails, catfish, painted buntings, scarlet tanagers, purple love grass, scrub oaks,
Carolina chickadees, redbuds, Indian paintbrush, orange spotted sunfish, prairie sumac,

Indian blankets, persimmons, witch grass, wild turkey, mesquite, bay breast warblers, canyon wrens, prairie roses & rugged rocks.

Daybreak on Mount Scott

On mornings like this I don't mind the fading out of the star-studded sky.
Gold lies ahead.
My friend and I love coming here outside of city noises.
As night turns to day, the creature I notice is the porcupine.
Indian blanket wildflowers will border the road in spring.
I speak of other places I've been, namely Paris and Stonehenge.
He speaks of the fifty familiar years in rhythmic pace.
This mountain speaks the language of the canyon wren and the elk's bugle.
The power of nature lies in its tender words and delicate touches.
On Mount Scott we walk in the land of new beginnings.
The jagged edges of broken tree limbs are last year's story.
Among these immense boulders every rule that defines a shape and a curve is broken.
Every day chances are taken.
I feel freedom in the air on mornings like this.

In This House

It is always spring or summer or autumn.

Soft-shelled pecans fill the yard in fall.
Purple irises in April frame the picket fence.
Summer breeds color. Hot pink knock-out roses.
Delicate fuchsia blossoms decorate the plant.
Bare feet are at ease on green velvet grass.
We sit under an orange and white umbrella sipping iced tea.

But you came in January when the nights are long,

When we need the warmth of handmade afghans, flannel robes, fireplaces,
When hot cocoa warms the hands after walking the dog,
When I read page after page curled up with the cat,
When the wind blows from the North,
And I light candles,
When I cook Provençal soup to serve with a crusty baguette.

Then it is spring and you say you will come again.

So I picture you in winter—
Newspaper spread on the bed,
Cooking a spicy chicken curry as
We slowly tear the piping hot naan.
You read a story to me and I listen,
And when you finish, I love you.

Now you are here, in summer, making a salad with prosciutto and radicchio.

I will tell you a story of the oryx,
An antelope with magnificent curved horns.
It was thought to be eradicated,
But it thrives and lives again.

Where will you be in the fall?

january 30, 2016

Bouquet of Basil

In the splendor of a black diamond watermelon summer
she grows mint, basil, oregano & thyme. She reaches for
his smile in the terra cotta pots of sage & parsley.

Five thousand miles away on a balcony above a cobblestoned street
she feasted on tomatoes, basil, garlic with pasta & parmesan. She
chose a rosé for their outdoor summer meal. Jeff Buckley's *Honeyman*
hummed through the opened door. Evening faded on Arndt Strasse.

Now it's a different summer night. Temperatures rise during
Oklahoma summers. Divine herbs still thrive in the fiery weather.
She picks the basil. A big bouquet. She breathes in the scent. Fresh like
an early morning rain shower on the way to Grand Canyon
    a fully bloomed rose *Honey Perfume*
        a coastal Baja breeze
            fern at the rainforest floor El Yunque, Puerto Rico
                crystal bubbles from a waterfall Aguas Calientes
                    homemade bread just out of the oven
                        the pink rose in her kitchen window

Fresh are the piñones in the back of pickup truck on the road to Taos.
Garlic, basil, pine nuts & lemon.
In her house, it is the summer of pesto & love country.

Postscript: Dear Friends

"It's true that nothing in this world makes us so necessary to others as the affection we have for them."
—Johann Wolfgang von Goethe, *The Sorrows of Young Werther*

Three Women in a City of Water

At first we were heavy with talk of work and wanting,
but with every corner turned we became lighter with rhapsody.
We left behind stories that shaped our desire—

stories of dry prairie winds and the need for rain,
of western sunlight that warms the skin of dark scars—
to see what lies ahead on the broken cobblestones of Venice

where still rule the old, the aged,
where youth is on the other side of the bridge.
As we stepped through the narrow passageway of rare friendships,

we smiled, we sipped prosecco, we ate gelato—
stracciatella, castagna, frutti di bosco.
We mingled with the ghosts of countless Venetian lovers.

We were three women in a city of water
where the trickle of laughter seeps down the stone through the ages
and youth is on the other side of the bridge.

Whispers of Old Kyoto

Her name is Uemura. I think of clouds, cherry blossoms, a whisper, koi that glisten in the pond, a silk scarf. I see the wrinkles around her eyes. She is not the adorned geisha drawing attention on the street. She is loose black pants and a white cotton shirt. She is old Kyoto, unstrung fresh water pearls. Her ryokan is difficult to find, an unobtrusive hideaway. At night lanterns light the way. I arrive with my wheeled luggage, noisy on the stone pathway, slide open her front door to enter the inner sanctum—bonsai forest, a stone garden, a step up to a straw mat, a shelf for my well-traveled boots. Light filters through the slotted door. She offers slippers. I slide back another door— leave America and my cultural mirrors for awhile—Tonight I will sleep on tatami mats in a room without walls. Shoji screens will open to gardens of green and silver leaves. Tomorrow I will climb the stairs to Kodai-ji temple for moon viewing and walk the bamboo grove. When I leave I will take a photograph of Mrs. Uemura. She will hold her hand up to shade her eyes from the sun and in a quiet, tender voice she will whisper *sayonara*.

on the pathway
empty rickshaws
await passengers

Tears

for betty friedan
born feb. 4, 1921
died feb. 4, 2006

betty friedan is dead
yes, feb. 4, 2006 she died
on her birthday
at 85
how do we mourn
do we bake a cake
or burn our bras
do we blow out the candles
i don't dare
i want to put flowers on her grave
in brave bold pink
and hold on tight to her feminine mystique

i'm faded red
and brave bold pink
i am blue eyes
and small white breasts
i have fuchsia dreams
and sun in my skin
i'm a woman of all these colors
shy and bold
i'll wear no black veil
to hide these tears
i'll thank her for brave bold pink
betty friedan is dead

march 22, 2006

```
mixture                                                      slaves
   of                                                          as
     chopped                                               constructed
       apples                                               buildings
         walnuts                                            ancient
           cinnamon                                           of
             & wine                                         mortar
               >>                                        <<
                 >>                                    <<
                   >>                                <<
                     >>                            <<
                       >>                        <<
                         >>> like the <<<
```

dear friend
who
invited
me to share
in the Seder

turkey
with
matzo
stuffing
applesauce
chicken soup
with knaidel
steamed fish
with horseradish
flourless cake
tea

does
not
own
a
gun

Desert Nocturne

—for suzi

the crash was in the desert
where the palm trees grow.

people conversed quietly on porches,
friends lingered after the movie,
ambulance sirens were background noise.

i didn't know it would be so hard is what my sister said
ten years after losing her son.

i would give her satie's gymnopédie
and geronimo's warrior cry.
i want to tell her old stones in the desert
sparkle in the sun.

how does she pick up the pieces again?
what do I tell her about love?

i can tell her
   palm trees are beautiful.
   the desert is beautiful.
   the sand is warm.

in memoriam,
chad makalewena heiligman
february 26, 1973-may 12, 1997

Long Live Liberace

In love with Liberace like a carnival
of color in the bottom of the sea. You are
there Liberace on the rocky beaches.
You are your own stage
with a black piano and a silver candelabra.
Your ring is a shiny beaded turtle,
turquoise and orange, dropped from
an overstuffed beach bag.
I want to run fast like your fingers
playing Saber Dance on powdery sand.
Yes Liberace
last song on the piano pounded out
by hands playing Malagueña.
Encore Liberace
With one more grand finale—
Your mix of Moonlight
Sonata with How Insensitive goes together
like coffee and red velvet cake.
Bow Liberace
up down like the black and ivory keys you torch.
Tide recedes from the shore leaving an explosion of exquisite shells.

r.i.p. james bassel, the pianist
june 8, 1944-february 20, 2014

Herb Garden

Fresh mint explodes in the front porch flower pots. The spider plant brims over edgy with new growth. Salvia displays a deep purple paintbrush. Ah, the pale wonder of lavender. Summer and I love basil, thyme, oregano, rosemary, sage & Swiss chard that rejuvenate with every cutting. The porch faces east like a temple entrance welcoming sun. I relax on the wicker couch in bare feet with "Vant to Bite My Neck" color on my toes. Dream.

I climb to a rooftop in Marrakech. Minarets dot the skyline. I sip mint tea in a delicate glass on a shiny embossed gold saucer and stir with a spoon so small, it's doll-like. I smell the pure sweetness of tea.

I want to make tabbouleh with you, chop fresh mint, squeeze lemon, drizzle oil, laugh in the kitchen, lick the spoon.

Proust tells of these moments that cast their spell.

Reunión

A dream took me there on waves in the Caribbean.
I landed on a street of sand.
Willie, two years gone missing, but there he is—
curly ball of white French poodle, all this time with my parents
in their c.1985 living room, wagging his tail, prancing in and out the screen door.
My dad reading his newspaper with Willie by his side.
My mom sitting on the patio with coffee and Willie.
I want to thank them for taking care of him.
I'll bring them a café con leche from Mexico,
cinnamon sprinkled on top. And my father, sandales.
My mother, a huipil. We'll all sit around the table and talk.
Sun blooming through the bay window. Willie at our feet.
Like Luis Buñuel, I'll zoom in to film the final scene of my dream.

Am I Blue?

Am I Blue?
Buffalo drum.

Cry a Billie Holiday landscape
between a black diamond watermelon & scrub oak leaves.

Blood oranges squeezed.
Honeybees.

Among boulders
hikers take a breath. [Broken-in boots & sweaty brows]

Am I Blue?
Buffalo drum.

Praise for wild food—
prickly pear cactus   persimmons   onions   & black walnuts

A nine-banded armadillo scuttles away—
creature of armor, long claws, 100 teeth.

Western diamondback blends in with the grass.
Sun beats down \ \ \

Am I Blue?
Buffalo drum.

In a Chagall Painting

Chagall, you took me off the interstate.
You led me to a blue highway.

After miles on I-40 with silver semi-trucks,
where cars pushed for Flagstaff before nightfall,
where faded billboards promised good food down the road,
I was longing for the fruit stand I had passed hours ago
that offered peaches,
the orange nectar of summer.

The next day
I was heading to Taos on highway 76,
winding through Chimayo, Las Trampas, Truchas,
where I saw clouds unfolding,
gathering momentum,
a story brewing in the big sky.

Chagall, you stirred up the accumulated dust
with heavenly rain. You washed away
the daily decorum of tailored suits
and gold-studded earrings. You buried
concrete parking lots under atmospheric skies
You dotted the landscape with *Ojo Sarco*
and golden shrubs of Chamisal.

Chagall, of all the animals you chose *le Coq,*
the soft feel of his feathers,
the piercing stare of his black eye.
You revealed the veiled woman
who once danced in Havana and
wore a flower in her hair,
her shoulder and arms bare.

Inside the *coq* you placed a couple.
How delicately you brushstroked their embrace.

Your story will never end.
You gave me clouds, forests, high road villages & sunsets.

Chagall, you took me off the interstate.

As a native of Southwest Oklahoma, **Patricia Bassel** loves open spaces and blue skies. Traveling and taking long walks are two of her passions, more specifically walking the city of Paris and walking her rescue dog Sappho. Her mother and father had a bookshelf full of books about local history including *The Way to Rainy Mountain* by N. Scott Momaday and *Geronimo* by Angie Debo. She grew up with a keen sense of place but also had a wanderlust spirit. She fulfilled her dream of becoming a French teacher and teaching abroad but never lost her love of Oklahoma and the Great Plains. She presently resides in Lawton, Oklahoma where she enjoys hiking the Wichitas, sometimes with Sappho and other times in the company of friends.

www.ingramcontent.com/pod-product-compliance
Lightning Source LLC
Chambersburg PA
CBHW030225170426
43194CB00007BA/868